i

Steve Jobs: The Man Behind the Bitten Apple

Steve Jobs: The Man Behind the Bitten Apple

Insight into the Thoughts and Actions of Apple's Founder

JR MacGregor

Steve Jobs: The Man Behind the Bitten Apple

Insight into the Thoughts and Actions of Apple's Founder

Published by CAC Publishing LLC.

ISBN 978-1-948489-84-3 paperback

ISBN 978-1-948489-83-6 eBook

Make sure to check out the other books in this 'Billionaire Visionaries' series:

Jeff Bezos: The Force Behind the Brand

Elon Musk: Moving the World One Technology at a Time

Bill Gates: The Man Behind Microsoft

Jack Ma: A Lesson in Trust, Honor, and Shared Prosperity

Richard Branson: The Force Behind Virgin

This book is dedicated to those of us who use Apple products daily and who have been impacted by the technological genius that was Steve Jobs.

Contents

Preface

We read biographies to learn about ourselves, not to pay homage to the subject. We study how others have tackled this world we live in so that we can make some sense of the curve balls thrown at us and of the failures of our own ambitions to take off. At other times, we reach out to biographies for inspiration and direction. The reasons we seek out the illumination of a soul that has passed before us are as varied as the lives we lead. What matters is not the reason we come to the table, but that we come at all.

If there is only one person you read about in your life, it should be this man, Steven Paul Jobs. If you haven't yet read anything about him, this book will serve as a good place to start; if you have already read about him, then this book will guide you toward a deeper insight.

This book is not about the who, the where, and the why. It's not about the how Steve Jobs was born, what school he went to, or the particularities of his life. A lot of that information is freely available on the Internet.

Instead, this book is about the leadership skills that Steve Jobs had, and the game he played and showed the rest of us how to play. This book should give you insights you can take away from looking at what made Steve Jobs unique, insights that will help you to blow up your own corner of the world.

Introduction

"I want to put a ding in the universe."

Steve Jobs

Think of Steve Jobs and the ubiquitous bitten apple comes to mind. Think of the Apple Computer, the iPhone, or the iPad, and the larger-than-life Steve Jobs comes to mind. They are indeed inseparable in the collective mind of this generation.

This book cuts through the hyperbole and anecdotes to find the true spirit of a man who captured the imagination of a nation through the vision he left behind, and who redefined the world in a variety of ways for different people. For the man on the street, Jobs redefined expectations of consumer electronics by bringing superior designs and intuitive user interface standards to the market and making those the norm. As a business professional, he demonstrated the unique ability to see things from both the macro perspective and the micro perspective.

There are a lot of misunderstandings about the way that Jobs did things, and many expectations directed toward him because of the myth that rose up around him. Steve Jobs may have looked and acted like a regular guy who sometimes walked bare foot in the conference room or bare foot on the grass outside, but to judge him by the standards of a regular guy would be a mistake. On a closer look, Steve Jobs was anything but a 'regular guy.' While he may have been humble and reverent, he was an exceptional man.

Studying the great men of history, you find that no two are alike in their achievement, but all of them have one thing in common – their inspiration is more than what the brain can ordinarily conjure. Their inspiration is almost divine, from Einstein's black holes, to Alexander the Great's ability to battle and bring communities together, from Newton's understanding of gravity, to Ford's assembly line that revolutionized personal transport.

To understand the workings of Steve Jobs' mind, you need to look at each individual aspect of his actions and trace the threads as they manifest through who he was, weaving together to form the person of Steve Jobs. I've tried to condense the observations I've made about this man's life, the movements he sparked, and the ideas he spread, and attempted to prioritize them in a way that will not only help you, the reader but will also pay homage to the man we are seeking to understand better.

To start with, Jobs had the ability to achieve such a deep focus that nothing else going on around him could penetrate the wall around his mind and attention. It wasn't until he finished what he was doing mentally that he would emerge to give his time to whomever or whatever demanded his attention in the outside world. He wasn't being arrogant when he stood silent as someone tried to engage him, he was just not present while he worked things out inside his own mind.

Steve Jobs is a giant among men not just because he created the world's most valuable company (by market capitalization), but also because he raised the standards of what we expected things to be and changed the way we did things. If you think of Steve Jobs just as a man who built computers, you'd be wrong. If you think commercialized computers, you'd be right, but you still wouldn't have encapsulated his contribution to this world. It isn't until you realize that Steve Jobs' contribution spanned across technology, entertainment, design, functionality, publishing, music, and hardware that you will begin to gain an insight into the expansive way his mind operated.

Because of Steve Jobs' influence, there is more to Apple than a computer, or a tablet, or a phone. Apple is about the way we, as humans, interact with technology, and how the standards Jobs established help us to conquer that technology to do things for us – without the frustration and intimidation that lesser products often produce.

Steve Jobs wasn't just an innovator. He was also an inspiration for those who want to break out of the mold of mediocrity. Some would argue that Steve Jobs' effect on those around him was the consequence and natural unfolding of his perfectionism. But it's never just one thing that drives a person. There is always a balance of forces that makes the actions of a man speak only of him for that moment in time. Once that moment passes, the man himself changes, and becomes a new man in a new moment.

The final analysis of a man should not be one that points to the aggregate of his actions to arrive at a mathematical average of his contribution. How could that be fair or accurate? Instead, the true measure of the man, a measure that excludes bias and envy, should be formed on the trajectory and intention demonstrated over the course of his life, giving weight to the areas of his life that touched the life of others. When you look at Steve from that perspective, what you find is a man who did not start off as someone who wanted to change the world, but as someone who wanted to have an impact in whatever way he knew how.

For those who think of Steve Jobs as a hardware genius, I hate to tell you this, he wasn't. For those of you who think that he was a software genius, I hate to tell you as well – he wasn't. He didn't invent the Internet like Sir Tim, he didn't create an operating system, and he didn't create anything physically tangible.

What he did do was to rethink the way we did things, how we saw things, and the standards we use to experience things. Steve Jobs took the computer from something that was, until then, a big, clunky machine for office and professional use, and had Woz redesign it for personal use. It was Woz that was the technical brains behind Steve Jobs. iTunes was born in response to Apple being left out of the music revolution when music was still just the ability to play a CD on a personal computer. Rather than falling behind and screaming "Me Too," Jobs didn't just install a CD player/burner on the Mac. Instead, he created iTunes so that all the music you wanted could be shared between devices, and there would be no need to burn the disk and play it on something else. It was an elegant solution to a growing problem.

When Jobs saw the invention of the mouse and the ability to use a GUI (Graphical User Interface) to operate a computer, he latched on to it to make the computer more user friendly. He took existing ideas and made them better and cheaper so that the man on the street could use those advances in technology. Jobs didn't invent any of these things – he just made them so that we could use them. He made it so that you and I, not just scientists in lab coats, could use them, and we didn't need to sell the farm to get one.

Steve Jobs made things relatable; he made things so that they would make sense to us. So, in a way, he may as well have been the inventor behind many of the things that have changed our lives, because he was able to look at those things and simplify them to make them relatable.

Jobs' idea of simplicity was not about dumbing things down. He didn't have a disparaging view of society; he had an appreciation - the kind an artist has while still seeking to elevate what the audience experiences. For Jobs, simplicity was not about shunning things that were not simple, it was about conquering complexity. To master complexity, you have to face it and tame it. The lion tamer doesn't exchange his whip and chair for a gun to destroy the lion, nor does he trade his lion for a cat to avoid the challenge. Instead, the lion tamer learns how to master the lion, just as Steve Jobs mastered the complexity of existing technologies for us.

Jobs' idea of simplicity didn't arise from being a simple man. Quite the contrary, Jobs was a complex individual, with complex thought processes, who was able to simplify the complex.

Chapter 1 Focus

"We don't get a chance to do that many things, and everyone should be really excellent. Because this is our life. Life is brief, and then you die, you know? So this is what we've chosen to do with our life."

Steve Jobs

Steve Jobs began a life not much different than most of us are presented with when we first gain a conscious appreciation of the world around us. Steve Jobs considered his adoptive parents, Clara and Paul Jobs, to be his only parents. He hardly acknowledged his biological parents who conceived him out of wedlock. They had given him up for adoption at birth due to the strict catholic views of his maternal grandparents.

Steve Jobs' rise to greatness can be attributed to his ability to focus and weed out distractions. During his early years, Jobs faced challenges with controlling his thoughts. To understand the level of focus that Jobs was ultimately able to achieve, you need to look toward his background in meditation and the lengths he went to in order to develop his ability to focus.

Many who are creative and driven tend to have a multitude of voices in their heads, pulling them in many different directions, making them want to do many things at the same time. These are the folks that have some of the best abilities to multi-task, but that ability is an illusion. Multi-tasking can seem superhuman in the beginning, but over time it wears you down and it causes you to be less than effective.

Steve Jobs was so filled with ideas and thoughts of his 'destiny' and mark on the world that his mind was a noisy place. To combat this, Jobs sought out ways to help him bring these thoughts under control. Jobs was not crazy, though some people equate having thoughts running in different directions as craziness. Nor, on the other extreme, was he superhuman, although he eventually became capable of an intense level of focus that almost seems superhuman.

Like Jobs, most people who are highly successful seem able to focus to the point of not being mentally present in the space they occupy physically. The ability to focus on one matter at a time and to be inspired by what is at hand is something that escapes most of us because we are not, consciously or subconsciously, able to be comfortable in the moment we occupy. There is always some form of distraction that becomes the excuse to move away from what we have otherwise deemed important.

There are two main things that cause distractions in our mind, and Jobs certainly battled at least one of these, although which one is not totally clear. The first are the competing thoughts that distract from other thoughts. This is common to many intelligent and creative people. There are many instances that seem to provide evidence that this was Jobs' issue. From his early days, he had so many competing thoughts that he struggled to find the path he so desperately needed.

This type of distraction usually occurs when you have an inspiration concerning something you are working on, and, as that thought develops, you become immersed in it and start to expand on it. That all works great until you get another great thought, and then you have two thoughts competing for your attention. This eventually becomes an avalanche of distraction. This type of distraction can typically be straightened out by the power of meditation. The key is to know that it is a distraction.

California in the seventies had a growing counter culture with a lot of talk about meditation and experimenting with drugs that took the mind to different states of consciousness. The era influenced several great thinkers, including Richard Alpert, who experimented with LSD and the power of meditation and transcendence. Richard Alpert, later known as Ram Dass, wrote *Be Here Now* about his travels in India and his discovery of life, meditation, and the inspiration of the soul. The book would become a beacon and guiding light for the young Steve Jobs who was looking to make sense of his divergent and competing thoughts.

When Steve Jobs was 19, he travelled to India, on a quest to meet with a Hindu guru named Maharaji, the same guru who had inspired and taught Ram Dass, the author of *Be Here Now*. The meeting never took place, but it was during that trip that Jobs would find the spark that eventually grew into a flame, becoming the source of his wisdom, the inspiration of his genius, and the foundation of his art.

Jobs ultimately embraced Buddhism more than Hinduism. In fact, Steve Jobs and his wife were married in a Buddhist ceremony, and his practice of meditation and Zen were more based on Buddhist principles and teachings.

In a sense, it is possible to see, in the way Jobs approached the tangible things of life, an integration of the power of that mindfulness and meditation into everyday high technology. This does not come from mere tinkering, only from being truly inspired. His designs, be it the iPhone or the iPad, were works of absolute sophistication.

Most importantly, meditation and mindfulness helped Jobs achieve a level of focus unlike any he had previously experienced in his life, and formed the basis for his ability to focus in on his thoughts and cut out the noise. He continued to develop this further as he got older and practiced it increasingly.

Ultimately, one of Steve Jobs' core skills was his ability to focus on exactly what was necessary, chiseling away and discarding everything else. I once heard him speak shortly after returning to lead Apple. The company was still in the mess it had found itself in during Jobs' absence, and people were regularly asking Jobs why Apple had stopped doing particular products and why they were not moving forward with certain areas of the business. The simple answer from Jobs was that focus is about saying no. Hearing that changed something deep within me.

"Focus is the ability to say no." Now think about that for a minute. Jobs was absolutely right. Our minds are built in such a way that we get random inspiration from every direction, by association, by triggers, by seeing something. Ideas pop into your head from everywhere, all the time.

And it's not just the thoughts that pop into your head, there are a myriad of other distractions that present themselves to us, especially today, with tweets, updates, and Instagram photos. Everything is beeping and buzzing away at your hand-held device or your tablet. Messages and phone calls come in, and there are ever more distractions at all hours of the day, at work, at home, even while you sleep. The only way to actually get something done is to say no.

Jobs developed the ability to look at things in strategic way and consider whether "the total was less than the sum of the parts." That was one of his engines of focus. When he looked at something and the yield was less than the vision, he would drop it. Many of the ideas pursued by the capable engineers at Apple, in the early days or during Jobs' absence from the company, were quickly axed when they didn't pass this test because of the quality of focus Jobs had developed over time.

Steve Jobs was a man who understood the difference between what is important and what seems urgent. Whether it's a distraction or an opportunity, if your plate is already full, the ability to say no is the foundation of your ability to focus.

Chapter 2 Taking Responsibility

"And no, we don't know where it will lead. We just know there's something much bigger than any of us here."

Steve Jobs

Steve Jobs possessed a unique characteristic above and beyond many in the same category, whether in Silicon Valley or among entrepreneurs generally, in wanting to take responsibility for more than what people were asking of him. When he looked at the interaction between his consumer and his product, he saw something that most designers or CEOs still don't fully appreciate. He saw the user experience in an atypical way from other industrial engineers. Rather than just simplifying something, he wanted the result to be a seamless integration. That kind of mindset set the stage for products that rolled out almost seamlessly and performed better than anyone ever expected.

Jobs believed that there shouldn't be a distinguishing demarcation between where the user's hand ended and the Apple product began. He knew that to be able to make everything simple, every single product they offered needed to integrate forward, backward, and sideways, in every way possible that so a user could pick up any one of his Apple products, put it down, and then pick-up another without changing one speck of his life. This is one of the reasons why your Mac can be your base station while your iPod plays your music. When they developed iTunes, the whole idea was to have these hardware devices be on the go. That idea revolutionized the way we saw hardware, and it created a new demand on the way we stored our content. It changed the face of functionality.

For this approach to work, and for the hardware to integrate seamlessly, Steve Jobs had to take end-to-end responsibility. Which he did. Not only did he take on all of the design and aesthetics, he went in deeper to understand how he could bring all the hardware elements together and tie them up, so that, at the touch of a button, everything was laid out for the user to experience. Due to Steve Jobs' vision, I can now whip out my iPhone and continue watching the movie I left off yesterday on my Apple TV. Because of his ideas, I can upload my documents from my iPhone, and then go onto my MacBook and retrieve them. The seamless integration of the different pieces of hardware was the direct result of Steve Jobs' refusal to accept less when he took on the responsibility for what he designed.

Steve Jobs wasn't looking at what he did from the perspective of profit. Profits were not his guiding motivation. Instead, he took end-to-end responsibility for the user's experience, and that would eventually make Apple one of the most profitable, wealthiest and largest companies on the face of this planet. Steve Jobs was playing the infinite game.

In the analysis of finite and infinite games, there are two kinds of leaders. One leader goes from quarter to quarter, jumping on every technological advance their competitors make. The other takes his company, regardless of what everyone else is doing, and moves forward. From only one perspective does the infinite player move – and that is the quest for an unprecedented standard of perfection. In the case of Steve Jobs, his focus was on the consumer and how to make lives better. In the infinite game Steve Jobs played, he did not follow the rules others played by when they followed the profits from quarter to quarter. When Jobs saw a technology that he didn't have, he didn't simply copy what others already had. Instead, he went the one step further.

When the Mac came out, it didn't come with a CD drive. So, when everyone else had CD drives, the Mac was left out of that game. Jobs was completely baffled that he had not seen it. But he didn't just decide that the next version of the Mac would come with a CD-ROM so that people could burn music and take it with them. Instead, he decided to give them the seamless integration that would eventually become iTunes. With that, he put Apple back out in front again, and, in so doing, he revolutionized the industry. No longer did you need to burn a CD or copy your music to a portable media player to take your music with you. All you needed was a strong and stable Internet connection to be able to automatically synchronize all your devices.

That was how Steve Jobs responded to a situation where he felt left behind. He didn't just jump in line and copy others. It would have been the easiest thing in the world to go to his vendors and ask them to design a CD-ROM to fit the Mac platform. Instead, he revolutionized the music and movie industry by taking responsibility from end-to-end for the user experience. That reveals a man who viewed his space in this world differently than the way an average person views theirs.

Ultimately, Jobs strove to take responsibility in all aspects and at all stages of everything he touched, from start to finish. He didn't just want to come in in the middle, do a small part, and take the credit. One of the things Jobs was very proud of was that Apple controlled both the hardware and the software. Neither was licensed out to intermediate vendors to do with as they wanted around the software; people could not just pick the hardware and install any software or operating system they wanted. Jobs provided an end-to-end solution and stood as a guarantee to say, *"this will work, and if it doesn't I will fix it."*

There would be no passing of the buck when a problem arose. Hardware vendors didn't have the opportunity to blame it on a software problem, and the software guys could not pass it off as a hardware problem. When you take responsibility, the only promise is that it works, no excuses.

When I try to look at my own life through the lens of how Steve Jobs looked at his, I don't find myself wanting to copy his life and what he did. I don't want to go out and make the next iPad or build the next Apple. What his example does make me want to do is to take stock of the way I do things in my own corner of the world. His example causes me to reflect on the way that I see and analyze things and what I prioritize. Do I tie my goals together in a harmonious way? Or do I prioritize my goals just to get a higher quarterly result?

This is a man that took over the responsibility of being able to provide the simplicity and the functionality of the products that he saw lacking. He decided early on that if he could do this, the profits would follow, but if he chased after the profits, all this would sink. He was right. Once while Steve Jobs was out of Apple for a time and the company was run like any other Fortune 500 company, chasing the bottom line from one quarter to the next, Apple fell. It took the return of Steve Jobs to the company he founded to turn it around, back to his original vision. Now, Apple continues to follow that vision, years after Jobs has passed on.

Chapter 3 Simplify

"I'm an optimist in the sense that I believe humans are noble and honorable, and some of them are really smart. I have a very optimistic view of individuals."

Steve Jobs

If focus was Steve Jobs' blueprint, then simplicity was his path. His brand of simplicity is unlike anything I've encountered in the other great men I've studied. Everything around Jobs was analyzed down to its most effective components, whittled down to the point where functionality and effectiveness increases substantially.

Most people misunderstand simplicity, particularly Apple's brand of it, as a lack of complexity. There may be some truth in that, but, for Steve Jobs, simplicity was not the avoidance of all things complex. Instead, it was in the conquering of what was complex in his daily life and in the products that he eventually engineered with intuition and emotional sensitivity that you find the ability to create products that intuitively transcended the inherent complexity of technical matters.

If you look at other technology companies, whether it's Dell, Microsoft or Compaq, in each, there is an air of unfamiliarity and unnecessary complexity. It almost represents a foreboding corporate structure that denies the pleasure of simplicity. It really puts the word 'hard' in hardware. With Apple, you don't find that. You see a device that is user-friendly. And because of that, Apple and Steve have been able to transcend, from computers to communication, to smartphones, to movies, to tablets and music.

When my son was three years old, he stood in front of an iPad at the Apple store and looked at it for the first time. He instinctively knew how to tap the home button to activate the device, and soon maneuvered his way around the main menu. It is both a testament to how smart children are these days and to how something as complex as a high-tech device can be designed to overcome unnecessary complexity. That is Steve Jobs' lasting legacy. That is what Apple has grown to embody. And that is what Apple's brand promise has continued to signify.

The common thread that runs through all the things Steve touched is not computers, but rather consumer goods and services enhanced through the use of technology. The intersection of tech and services empowered people to take their efficiencies to the next level. It empowered the consumer to go about their daily lives and to do it in style. People buy iMacs for two reasons: iMacs are powerful enough to sit at home as their base station to play games, download music, and enjoy movies on their stunning screens, and iMacs are attractive because they are aesthetically pleasing. On one hand, Steve Jobs empowered the consumer, while on the other, he put them at ease.

There is a story that makes its rounds on the Apple campus. It seems that when the Macintosh was being designed, one of the designers had included a handle for the top of the computer. Keep in mind that this was a solid piece of desktop machinery. Production engineers cried out at the added manufacturing expense, arguing that it was not worth the price because the handle wouldn't do anything for the computer since the Macintosh was designed to sit on top of a desk and stay there. And, truly, during the time I owned my own Macintosh, it sat on my desk, and I never once moved it until I replaced it. Yet, when Jobs saw that handle, he instantly insisted that the handle remain. He instructed the engineers to do whatever they had to do to make it possible.

What Steve Jobs recognized in that handle was the ability to change the mindset of consumers who, at that time in 1984, looked at computers as something forbidding. Computers, back then, were designed to sit in rooms, like the minicomputers and the supercomputers that had required large dedicated spaces. The mere idea of a computer intimidated people. Adding that handle empowered a person psychologically by communicating that he would be able to lift that computer up and walk away with it. That gave the ordinary person power over the computer.

On the screen and inside the computer, many other changes had also taken place. The computer now had a graphical user interface that allowed regular people to sit down and intuitively click on what they needed. You didn't need a manual to tell you what to do. You could look at it, move the mouse around, and figure out how to get on your way. You could click on it the same way my three-year-old was able to maneuver his way around the iPad the first time he laid eyes on it.

Simplicity is a curious thing. Einstein once said that things should be made as simple as possible, but not simpler. Steve Jobs personified this idea in his life and in his vision.

Simplicity is not about shying away from matters that are complex. It's about conquering complexity. Jobs' practice of simplicity was to tear down anything that didn't make sense or didn't need to be there until he reached the point where it wouldn't benefit from being simplified any further.

We can all find out how to master complexity, but Steve Jobs did it for us by designing products that, while enormously complex in the background, don't seem complex to us at the point of use. You don't need to know how the operating system runs a computer in the background for you to be able to effectively use the computer. When you click to open an app, you don't need to know the list of subroutines that causes the computer to activate, or how the microprocessors bring about other actions. You just need to know that when you click something, it opens, and it's ready for you to use. And this happens seamlessly and intuitively.

During the design process for the iPod, Steve Jobs was in a meeting where they were working on the design of the user interface and the way users would get their music to come up. Already months into it, they had a comparatively complex process where the user had to enter the menu and look for an answer, searching slowly, making his way down through different directories. Despite all the work that had already gone into the development of the iPod, Steve Jobs decided that it wasn't elegant and decided to tear down anything and everything that did not sit well with him. His benchmark was simple – he wanted users to be able to get to the music they wanted to listen to in three steps from wherever they were on the iPod. That was an extremely tall order. But eventually the design process stopped and everyone realized that it was the right thing to aim for.

Jobs even looked at the power button and questioned its existence in his effort to make the iPod more intelligent. The designers were stunned but came to realize that he was right. The on/off button was indeed obsolete, and they designed the iPod without the need to have an on/off button.

I remember my own first iPod and the first time I realized there was no power button. I was flabbergasted because I had been frustrated from all the times I had to turn things on to use them. Eventually, as old habits wore off, I realized how simple life became when you didn't have to turn a device off and it just came back on whenever you picked it up.

Apple has continued to follow that legacy of simplicity in their introduction of new products, especially the new iPhone X. The technology behind the product is of no concern to the consumer. What matters is how it works for them. Apple continues to create products that follow the essence of Steve Jobs' genius of simplifying things for us.

Chapter 4 Drive

"Woz is living his own life now. He hasn't been around Apple for about five years. But what he did will go down in history."

Steve Jobs

No matter what the person's ability to inspire the imagination or their ability to think of solutions, without the drive to lift a finger, none of that intangible thought is going to matter. In Steve Jobs' case, he had the passion and the drive to push things beyond human limits. Steve Jobs certainly wasn't superhuman, but he does show us that the ability to drive one's self is within us all. It just depends how far we are willing to take it. Jobs sought to take it as far as possible.

Each successful person has a different way to energize their own march toward success. Some are driven by profits, some by fame, and some by the simple and pure satisfaction of accomplishment. There are others who just get to work doing what they feel to be their best at that moment, and once they have achieved their best for that goal, they move on to something else. They get up and build a computer. Then they get up to build a phone, and when that phone is done, they move on to build an iPad. When that iPad is done well, they just keep building more things to elevate the human experience. And that was the sort of man that Steve Jobs was.

But what really drove him? What was the force that kept driving him whether in the face of defeat or illness? What was it that drove him toward his goals, and to have one goal after another? How did he fire up his focus or his ability to bend reality?

Steve Jobs, and probably other thought leaders and industry titans, seems to have had an ability to bend the reality of those around them – and thereby bending physical reality for all of us. Jobs was able to shift the sense and perception of reality of his colleagues and business partners by driving them purely on the energy flowing from his words. Jobs screamed at, tormented, and pushed his workers and colleagues even to the point of exhaustion. His colleagues called it the "Reality Distortion Field."

It was widely known on the Apple campus that Jobs could literally warp the reality around him. The phrase "Reality Distortion Field" used to describe Jobs' ability to alter average reality was taken from the Sci-Fi show Star Trek. (All the engineers and people who work at Apple, including Steve Jobs, are, to a certain extent, geeks.) This reality distortion field was pretty much an ongoing thing that altered the way you would see things. It could be argued that Jobs had the same effect on the rest of the world too. Before, there were no sleek lines; there were no iPads. Jobs changed our reality. He distorted it, and, now, because of him, we demand a different kind of product instead of the old boxes. And we demand integrated solutions that complete our lives seamlessly.

There is a well-known story from the period when Steve Jobs was still with Atari, according to which his boss told him that if he could redesign one of the Atari products and simplify it using fewer parts so that it would cost less to make, Jobs would get a bonus. Jobs accepted the challenge and went to Steve Wozniak – the one with the technical brains behind the operation – and told Wozniak that if he could do this task there would be a bonus for the both of them. Jobs didn't mention the actual value of the bonus and told Wozniak that it was only a four-day deadline. Wozniak was certain he could never comply. In Wozniak's mind, the task would take a month, at the least, if not more. But Jobs jumped into his reality distortion mode and got Wozniak to sit down and focus. Low and behold, in just four days, Wozniak had managed to create a simpler version of Atari's hardware. Jobs had cut 26 days from Wozniak's original belief of how long it would take. That's some serious reality distortion and it is something that really works.

Steve Jobs' ability to change reality was a function of his enthusiasm, his sense of purpose, and his believability. Combined, they formed a formidable triumvirate of credibility that caused others to believe what they once could not. That kind of ability only comes when you have the belief yourself.

That ability to bend reality was something that Jobs applied to all situations, and often at Apple. Did he know a different reality, or did he deliberately distort the sense of reality to get others to follow? I'm convinced that it wasn't that he was deliberately distorting others' reality, it was that his own mental experience of reality was actually different.

I notice this same ability in the minds of other movers and shakers. I see it in the minds of up and coming entrepreneurs. I see it in thought leaders and product innovators. And it is different than what we see in the general population who are more followers than innovators. The thought leaders who can alter reality become the people we rely on to make our lives better and improve our tomorrows. These are the people that stand out as the finest examples of what humanity has to offer.

Steve Jobs was different from everybody else. If it weren't for his ability to bend reality and his ability to drive his staff, he would have been just another regular guy. But every single person who stood in the shadow of the Apple campus – everyone that had been in some way pushed and prodded and yelled at, even ones who left under less than perfect circumstances – would stand up to say that they were better off because of him, that they were able to produce a better quality product because of him.

As I look at Steve Jobs' life, I find myself asking, "What drives me?" The answers I come up with suggest that my life is as mediocre as the next person's because I keep doing what everybody else is doing. And yet my days are filled. To step out of a mundane existence of achieving small goals in small-minded ways requires a decision – a decision to change one's perspective on one's own life. To change what you can accomplish, to change what you want to accomplish is always based on a decision.

Steve Jobs decided early in his career that he was going to touch the lives of others by improving it in any way he knew how. That thought predated his viewing of Steve Wozniak's microcomputer – the circuit board that launched everything. Jobs already knew that he wanted to do something. He just didn't know what it was going to be. That's the reason he could jump from personal computer to cell phone, from hardware to software, from communication to entertainment. None of these, before Steve Jobs, had anything in common.

It wasn't until Apple that everybody realized the possibility of integrating hardware and software. Even Microsoft was purely an operating systems company before it went on to other software. Steve Jobs was criticized for not allowing the OS (Operating System) to be licensed on any other device built by third parties in the way Windows was. Although Windows is in 90% of the world's machines, Microsoft doesn't make 90% of the world's machines. Instead, Microsoft focused only on the operating system and licensed it out to whoever wanted it.

Microsoft was not in it for the experience; they were in it to expand their bottom line. They didn't look at the consumer as a person; they saw the consumer as a contributor to their bottom line. Steve Jobs looked at his consumer as a person who would have an experience with his product, and he wanted to take end-to-end responsibility for that. To do that, Jobs had to alter and reshape everyone else's reality through the sheer force of his drive.

Chapter 5 To Hell with Profits

"What we want to do is make a leapfrog product that is way smarter than any mobile device has ever been, and super-easy to use. This is what iPhone is. OK? So, we're going to reinvent the phone."

Steve Jobs

Steve Jobs' drive to focus on the product and make it work for the consumer meant that profits were not his first motive. Profits would come to Apple if they kept to his vision.

During the period that Steve Jobs left Apple, Apple tried the usual way of doing things, running Apple the way Fortune 500 companies are run, based on quarterly profits and annual targets, using the benchmarks used by every Fortune 500 company. Since they all used them, it had to be right. Right? But that didn't work for Apple.

Apple proved that it didn't work that way, and it began to fail. Steve Jobs had to come back to help his company grow again. And he did. He turned it around by bringing back his brand of focus, his brand of taking responsibility, and by simplifying matters. He drove his people to achieve perfection, and he said, "To hell with profits."

Whether at Apple or Pixar or anywhere else, the effect Steve Jobs had on those who worked with him or took direction from him can only be described as frustration. Regardless of the location, Steve was never known to be the easy on the people that worked on his products. It wasn't just the constant demands on their time or on their mental strength, it was also the fact that every time a project they were working on had advanced to the stated goal, Jobs would step in and take everything back to the drawing board. Jobs would feel that something had gone askew somewhere along the line, and he would not be able to accept it. That was just what he was like. It happened at Pixar during the making of Toy Story, it happened while designing the iPad, and it happened with the iPhone.

Every product that came out of Job's involvement faced this point of inflection. This was what would push him – his quest for perfection. Job's standards of perfection were beyond what anyone else could dream of coming close to.

One of these moments came during the development of the iPhone. The idea for the tablet had come first, and Steve Jobs' team had already begun developing the iPad when the idea to push the iPhone took priority. So, they put the iPad back on the shelf and redirected their resources toward developing the iPhone.

The iPhone was to be a game changer. It was designed to transform the way we interact with our cell phones, change how we see the entire experience, and change the relationship we have with our cellphones. The vision that Jobs had for the iPhone was extremely ambitious.

The iPhone was to change how we communicate by voice and text as well as how we interact with the Internet, and so the physical object - the tangibles – needed to symbolize the intangible. It was the herald of a new age, and so it was not going to be cast in plastic. It was set in an aluminum case and covered with glass.

One morning, during the late stages of design, Jobs put a stop to the process. He hadn't been able to sleep the night before because the design suddenly wasn't sitting well with him. There was too much aluminum case and too little glass. Instead of showcasing the phone, they were showcasing the case. Jobs wanted to turn that whole thing around. So, the designers of the iPhone and Jobs came together and rethought the concept and the aesthetics. It felt impossible because they were already running close to the deadlines to get production underway, but they still went back to the drawing board.

They needed to reduce the masculinity of the phone which had more case and less glass. They needed to get to that tipping point where the masculinity balanced the femininity, so the product would comfortably appeal across the board. As it stood, the aluminum overpowered any sophistication the phone might have had. It looked like an expensive brick, but a brick nonetheless. And so the perfectionist in Steve Jobs, fueled by the desire to connect technology to the human experience, took over and redesigned the phone so that you could look into a window of glass.

It became clear that everyone would need to stay weekends and nights to get the iPhone project back on track. And they did. As much as people complained about how much Steve Jobs demanded of them, they never sat back and declined his call to action. For Steve Jobs, it was one of his proudest moments not only because the product was brought to life, but also because he saw the people who worked at Apple come together as one seamless organization focused on one idea with one inspiration.

When Apple went back and resurrected the concept of the tablet to continue its development, Steve Jobs repeated the process, demanding perfection when he started to feel less than satisfied with what they had already come up with.

When the iPad came out and I purchased my first one, the thing my little boy noticed was how inviting it was to just grab it. I hadn't noticed that because I, too, would just grab it. One of the reasons why I chose the iPad over anything else was simply because it did not feel overbearing. Instead of using square edges on the iPad, Apple had tapered it. That tapering allows you to slide your fingers and grab it as you go. That made a big difference in the product's acceptability and in how it is used. It wasn't just something you could replace your laptop with. It created a new class of product.

Steve Jobs' genius was to make products that did more than their job; he made products that integrated with human psychology. He wasn't driven to make profits; he was driven to create perfection, and this made our experience better. If we want to emulate Steve Jobs, and change the world the way he did, we need to strive for that sort of perfection, not profits.

Chapter 6 Balance

"This revolution, the information revolution, is a revolution of free energy as well, but of another kind: free intellectual energy. It's very crude today, yet our Macintosh computer takes less power than a 100-watt bulb to run it and it can save you hours a day. What will it be able to do ten or 20 years from now, or 50 years from now?"

Steve Jobs

To many, Steve Jobs would not be considered an embodiment of balance, and, yet, I believe he had the concept of balance mastered, and that he was highly effective because of that. Just because someone is highly focused and excels at what they do doesn't necessarily mean they are out of balance in any way. In fact, I have argued to colleagues and friends for years now that the more balanced you are, the more you can do. Steve Jobs was the embodiment of this very concept - the ability to excel comes from the ability to balance. There are a couple of ways that we can look at this concept of balance.

First, balance is about centering, and focus is all about centering. We have already talked about Jobs' extraordinary ability to focus. To focus, you have to bring all your energies into balance so that you can occupy that single, central focal point that unites everything else. Too much of one thing throws your balance off, putting you too far from something else. Balance is a delicate state requiring the mental fortitude to hold disparate things together. Steve Jobs saw this balance in everything he did.

Jobs knew early on that there was more to this existence of ours than our intellect. He understood the value of meditation and mindfulness. He knew there was more to advancing our existence than achievement over a quarter or over a financial year. There was more to product engineering than refining something that already existed. There would always be a higher plateau to reach and a new horizon to move towards.

The most intriguing aspect of understanding Steve Jobs in terms of balance was his capacity to stand at the juncture of divergent areas, and remain comfortable with opposites and extremes. He could occupy the intersections of science and art, of creativity and engineering, and of humanity and technology. He became the nexus bridging the human experience with the technological revolution. Steve Jobs was our interpreter, and the only way you can be an interpreter is when you understand both sides of the story. You can't interpret something if you don't know half of it. Jobs was able to translate technology into the human experience. His creativity was not limited by science, nor was his scientific understanding limited by his ability to humanize it. This special ability to balance opposite ends of the spectrum elevated Steve Jobs above the pantheon of other successful men.

Although Jobs was at the forefront of technological innovation, he had the balanced perspective to understand that technology could not replace direct human contact, and that two souls collaborating could not be emulated online. Even though he was the creator of and inspiration behind high-tech electronic communication tools like the iPhone and the iPad, with their apps like iChat, Steve Jobs hardly used them himself if he had the option to stand directly in front of the person he needed to speak with. The creator of one of the most ubiquitous communication devices on the planet for this generation preferred to meet someone in person rather than chat or text.

Likewise, when Jobs created workspaces for his employees, he designed them to promote one-on-one meetings and impromptu discussions. When Pixar's new building was designed, Jobs made sure it was designed to promote direct person-to-person collaboration. When he wanted to get Corning to develop the glass screens for the iPhone, he went to talk with the Corning people in person. When he wanted to understand meditation and spirituality, he boarded a plane and travelled to India in person.

The second type of balance Steve Jobs exemplified was the ability to see both the forest and the trees. Most people see either the details or the big picture, but not usually both in a balanced way. Jobs was consistently able to see and balance the big picture with the minutest of details. To understand how rare a talent this is, consider what happens when two people, one who sees the big picture and the other who sees the details, try to collaborate. There are usually huge variations in perspective and objectivity, and often the conversation breaks down. That is the reason CEOs have difficulty speaking to bean counters, and why mid-level managers can't seem to get along with those who work the lines. It is always this breakdown not in communication but in perspective.

When you look at the human experience, we occupy the extremes of the spectrum, micro and macro. Steve Jobs was able to balance and function at both ends, and appreciate both. His balance was the result of repeated practice and an innate desire to look at things from the larger perspectives, to see the broad strokes, while drilling down to the smallest details to understand what he was doing. It is rare to find the capacity to balance both perspectives in one person. Jobs had the broader vision that great kings have but also had the ability to look at the immediate details that great soldiers have.

To conquer the world of business and make it big, we've been advised to see things from a holistic perspective, and we have gone on to think that 'holistic' means 'macro,' to see all things within one large frame. But that sort of overarching, wide-angle perspective tends to hide the details and obscure intricacies in a way that results in problems down the road.

Steve Jobs could develop an iTunes because he saw the transformation of an entire industry from a macro scale perspective. While his urgency may have been fired up by the Mac being left behind with the introduction of CD-ROMs, Steve Jobs' balanced perspective produced a solution that was elegant and shifted the ground under the entire industry and consumers alike. He was able to direct the development of the iPhone, seeing in its intricate features how those would relate to a tactile human experience, and seeing the details that would ensure the overall smoothness of its operation.

***

Chapter 7 The Game Steve Played

"There's no other company that could make a MacBook Air and the reason is that not only do we control the hardware, but we control the operating system. And it is the intimate interaction between the operating system and the hardware that allows us to do that. There is no intimate interaction between Windows and a Dell notebook."

Steve Jobs

As a student of the psychology of success, I frequently analyze the nature of men's actions on their routes to significant achievement and lasting legacy. Sometimes, I begin my analysis during a person's teenage years, as I did with Elon Musk and his rise from middle-class roots in South Africa. In some cases, I look at the beginning of a man's career. I've also looked at the life of someone like Jeff Bezos beginning when he first got to New York after completing his education at Princeton. I use a variety of different frameworks to try and comprehend the complex actions and the even more complex thought that may have been going on in the minds of my subjects. They may not be completely accurate frameworks, but they come close to placing each person in a context where we can identify their unique ability so that we may cultivate it, and the world can be a better place for it.

In the case of Steve Jobs, the framework I have found most useful to understand my subject is game theory. I don't mean the game theory developed to help us identify optimal situations. I'm talking about the game theory designed to look at men according to the games they play in the work they do – the finite game and the infinite game. If you have read some of my other books, you may have encountered this type of analysis done on other subjects I have observed. For those who aren't familiar with this framework, let me briefly take you through it.

There are only two kinds of games in anything you do. One is the finite game and the other is the infinite game. In a finite game, you play to get to a finish line that is determined in the short term. The only objective is to win – the only object is to vanquish the opponent. The time horizon is short, and it's like playing a game of chess. The whole point of the match is to vanquish the opponent and to do it within the time it takes to complete a certain objective or to run down the clock.

The infinite game is nothing like a finite game because the objective of the infinite game is the exact opposite of the finite. While the finite game is designed with the purpose of winning a limited game, the purpose of the infinite game has nothing to do with winning or losing. The goal of the infinite game is to keep the game going.

For those familiar with the eighty's movie 'War Games,' you may remember that the computer decided to play tic tac toe and to use the same logic in a simulated thermonuclear war. The computer, Joshua, gamed out each scenario according to the strategies available to it, and considered the range of its opponent's possible responses. When you play only one game and the objective is to win, but there is the chance of losing, it is okay to go all out and expend all of your artillery, use all of your strategies, and exhaust all of your supplies in pursuit of that ultimate win. Once you have won or lost, the objective of the game has been reached.

But what happens when the game is not designed to be won, but to continue indefinitely? That is when you have the infinite game.

Finite games are played by finite players. Infinite games are played by infinite players. If only more understood the type of neural wiring they have – whether they are more suited to finite games or to infinite games – you would see more people who are extremely successful because success is not defined by whether you play the finite or the infinite game, but by whether or not you play the game you were built to play.

If a finite player plays an infinite game, he will lose. You can see why. A finite player will be trying to win for that quarter or that year, and if he uses finite strategies to win a game designed to be played over and over, he will exhaust his resources and have nothing to show for it. On the other hand, if he is an infinite player but playing a finite game, each game will render him a loser, and he will eventually exhaust his psychological frame.

On the other hand, when a finite player plays a finite game, his true opponent isn't another finite player, his opponent is success at large. The same applies to the infinite player; when the infinite player plays an infinite game, his opponent is not another infinite player, it is also success at large. When a finite player tunes his resources and plays that finite game, he triumphs. When an infinite player plays an infinite game, he also emerges victorious, given the right set of circumstances.

With this cursory understanding of the finite in the infinite game framework, we can look at Steve Jobs according to this context. Considering Jobs in both scenarios to identify whether he is a finite or an infinite player, I find that he is well adapted and well suited with his skills to be an extremely formidable infinite player. And that is what you see – not only in the person of Steve Jobs but also in the company he founded.

Apple, whether they realize it or not, is still playing the infinite game. Apple builds products that transcend today's fads and temporary trends. They build products that are not designed to compete with its closest competitors but to completely conquer that technology, breaking out of the confines of short term competition.

For example, the latest release of an Apple product is the iPhone X. And the biggest, newest feature of the iPhone X is its facial recognition technology. The day after Apple's launch of the iPhone X, there was a lot of excitement on the internet from those in attendance at the launch. That excitement soon gave way to mockery in the forums and blogosphere as supporters of other manufacturers started to weigh in on the product. By the day after Apple made the announcement, many Monday morning quarterbacks were saying that Apple hadn't come up with anything new, arguing that facial recognition technology had already been in Android devices for a couple of years now. And this was true.

However, Apple's release of facial recognition technology hadn't been intended to compete with Android. Apple could have easily purchased or merged with a company that provided facial recognition technology during the same season that Samsung released its version. Emulating another company would have been easy, especially in this industry, but Apple didn't do that either in the same season or even during the following season. Instead of competing over short-term profits, Apple chose to go into research to develop the technology much further than what already existed in the marketplace.

You see, Samsung had been playing the finite game: this quarter, this result, they asked, "What can we put on the shelf that beats everything else, NOW!" It didn't matter that Samsung's facial recognition technology could be duped by a static image. You could use a photograph or even a 3D sculpture of the person's face, and the phone would unlock, spilling its information.

But you couldn't do that with the new facial recognition technology Apple developed because they had gone a few steps further in being able to map the face with special heat recognition technology. If you were to put a sculpture or a photograph in front of it, the phone wouldn't sense any heat from the sculpture, especially not the heat map of an individual's face, and it would not find the three-dimensional points that mapped the face using bifocal cameras. Instead of competing on what already existed, Apple redefined the game, breaking right out of its finite limits.

The point here is that one company, Samsung, plays a finite game, and does very well at it, while the other company, Apple, plays the infinite game, and does very well at it. Comparing the two would not be fair to either. You can't take Apple, following Steve Jobs' philosophy, and compare it against Samsung, with Samsung's philosophy, because each does well in their own type of game.

In the same way, you can't take two different leaders and compare them if they are wired to be two different kinds of players. Jobs, and those who follow his example, are infinite players because they play not to win in the short-term quarter but to make lasting change. When they achieve that lasting change, others come along to build upon it, developing it further – benefiting Apple as it sits on top of the redefined industry. Apple has no problem in playing that infinite game, because the company has mirrored the Steve Jobs legacy and personality extremely well.

Chapter 8 A Faster Horse?

"We're going to be able to ask our computers to monitor things for us, and when certain conditions happen, are triggered, the computers will take certain actions and inform us after the fact."

Steve Jobs

There are two kinds of leaders. The first type subjects his decision-making process to focus groups, public opinion, the opinion of the masses, and to the whims and fancies of fads. He seeks to see the trend in the fads, and he rides the leading edge of those trends to satisfy the popular view. This is the populist leader. In many cases, the populist leader is a finite game player.

The second type of leader is one who does not look toward the opinions of his customers or the masses but creates what is best for them. He is almost like a father creating what's best for his children. If children were allowed to choose their dinner, it'd most certainly be M&M's and

Skittles, but if the father chooses dinner, he chooses what is best for them in the long run. This is the infinite player.

Steve Jobs was famous for his refusal to be limited by what focus groups had to say about a product. He did, however, design products based on how the product would impact the life of the consumer. He was of the opinion that people don't really know what they want. This is much like the story often told of Henry Ford. When Ford was asked about how people would look at his product, his straight and resoundingly resolute answer was that, if he had left it up to the people, they would have asked for a faster horse. Instead of a faster horse, Ford gave the people an automobile – and changed the course of history. That's exactly how Steve Jobs approached things. He didn't seek the opinion of a consumer who wants a faster horse; he sought to define the consumer's opinion and make the consumer's life easier.

Previously, we talked about Jobs' ability to find a balance in looking at science and technology set against humanity, and to bridge these apparent opposites. But, in fact, Zen-like, Jobs did not actually see them as opposites. He saw with his intuition an all-encompassing ideal that takes everything as it is.

The universe is not built out of chemistry, physics and biology, cosmology, and astronomy. The universe is one big amalgamation of everything. In its Zen and Zen-like purposes, we find everything is what it is. There is no discipline that is separate from the rest. It is only broken down into digestible parts because our mortal minds can't find a way to absorb all of it at once. But there is a big picture, and there are some who can see it. In our generation, there are a few people with that ability, and one of them was Steve Jobs.

Jobs had the ability to see the big picture, as well as drill down to the details. He could appreciate the whole picture, and see where the small reacts with the small to create the big and see how the big interacts with each other to create the whole. That is what it's like to be inside the mind of an infinite player.

That is what it's like to be a leader. A leader who is an infinite player is a person who plays the long game, a person who looks to change things, not to keep up or keep ahead of trends. That is the kind of person we can trust to lead us. The other type of leader is not a person to lead us – that's just a person who satisfies our penchant for a quick fix.

A scene in a recent movie portraying Steve Jobs illustrates a quality that made me reevaluate my own way of doing things. In the scene, they were in Jobs' parents' garage trying to build the first Mac. Jobs looked inside the box at all the chips on the circuit board, and saw that all the chips were not properly arranged, so he mentioned it to his colleagues, including Wozniak, saying that he wanted those chips aligned and nicely arranged. Jobs' colleagues argued that no one was going to look inside the box. In the movie, Steve Jobs' answer was "They may not know, but I will."

Steve Jobs was more concerned with how he, himself, saw something than what others would think. When he took the responsibility to create something, he took full responsibility for it. Consequently, even if someone wouldn't see what was going on in the back end, he wanted to make it elegant. Apparently, he had learned this from his father, who was very good with his hands, with carpentry, mechanical work, and doing stuff around the house. Jobs' father had taught the young Steve that even when no one gets to see the back side of something, or the rear end of the fence, he would still know. His father told him that it didn't matter what other people got to see, what matters is what you get to see. That work ethic, that pride in what he did, and that knowledge of what went on behind the scenes was very important to the way the mature Jobs did things.

When you see everything, you see the big picture, you see the aesthetics of the lines on the outside, and you see what the chips are doing on the inside. That was quintessentially what Steve Jobs was all about. He didn't need focus groups to tell him what was good. He didn't need engineers to tell him that putting a handle on the top of a Macintosh was a waste of money. He didn't need bean counters to tell him that it wasn't how it should be done. It was by staying true to his own vision that he built a company from scratch to the point that it redefined how the rest of the world operates. His competitors run their businesses with the sole purpose of competing with the legacy Jobs left behind. They go to work every morning to try and beat Apple at the game Steve Jobs created. Jobs not only sparked a revolution, he was the revolution.

Conclusion

"Innovation distinguishes between a leader and a follower."

Steve Jobs

My entire motivation for reading about, studying, and observing men of significant success, and for talking to people who have left a formidable mark on this world, is to learn the lessons they can teach us. There are many reasons to inquire into the life of a man who has touched our experience in so many ways. From the way Steve Jobs could inspire us through his simplifications to the way he conquered complexity, we discover that we are capable of far more than what we witness and perform in our daily lives.

I have laid out this book very differently from other books I have written about men of great accomplishment. Over the past eight chapters, the goal has been to take one characteristic at a time and break it down to how and where it applied in Steve Jobs' life, and how or what resulted from it. To understand Steve Jobs, I broke down his way of doing things into eight categories, across those eight chapters, so that we could find inspiration and apply his way of doing things in our corner of the world.

We started by looking at one of the bedrock abilities of this man, his ability to focus on exactly what was necessary, chiseling away and discarding everything else. Jobs said, "Focus is the ability to say no." When there are so many distractions and opportunities clamoring for attention, the only way to actually get something done is to say no.

Second, we looked at the power of taking responsibility. When you take responsibility, whether it's for a mistake, or it's for a product you create, whatever you take responsibility for can flourish. Steve Jobs took responsibility for all aspects and stages of everything he touched, from start to finish. He made sure Apple retained control of both their hardware and their software, so that Apple provided an end-to-end solution with the promise that it would work, or they would fix it. No excuses.

Taking responsibility can convert even a mediocre act into a great legacy, and Steve Jobs took responsibility for everything, end-to-end, without any qualms whatsoever. Not only does Apple have control over the hardware it builds, and the software it writes, but it now also has control over the content that it distributes. How is that for end-to-end responsibility?

Third, we talked about simplification. How to simplify everything so that users don't have to be rocket scientists to operate the devices.

Look at any Apple product and you will find that there is significant technology behind those sleek lines and polished surfaces. Everything Jobs created stood at the intersection of high technology and practical usability for the average person. When you pick up your iPod, you don't need to worry if it's going to play, or if the touch sensor has enough tactile pressure to activate it, or if it even turns on. You know, after years of use, that whatever happens, it will work. That takes complex engineering behind the scenes and even higher standards of taking responsibility than you can imagine. When you pick up your iPad, the capacity for that iPad to function as you expect it to requires flawless engineering, foresight, and a strict adherence to standards.

Apple products remain as evidence of the man who created them. Whatever you think of Apple products, they reveal the handiwork of one man, and the integrity of his standards, and clarity of vision he had for simplifying complex processes. Everything from the Apple T.V. to the iPhone has been marked with Steve Jobs' signature vision, and by his care, patience, and determination to conquer the complexity of the technology and simplify the human interface with it to make devices easy to operate. You don't need to be able to understand programming to operate some of the most complex hardware in existence because of the standards that Steve Jobs stood for.

The fourth chapter talked about Jobs' ability to be driven. We looked at the factors that drove Steve Jobs and how he drove himself, taking ideas and incorporating them into the things he believed would make people's lives better. We also looked at how and why Jobs drove others relentlessly to succeed, but they loved him for it because he brought out the best in them.

We also looked at what he focused on in the product. He believed that the pursuit of profits was a worthwhile endeavor, but it was not the core of what he should focus on. Jobs believed if he focused on the product and made it work for the consumer, the profits would follow. He was right. As long as Jobs ran Apple according to his vision, it flourished to become as gargantuan it is today. Taking end-to-end responsibility, Steve Jobs drove his people to achieve perfection and simplicity, and said, "To hell with profits."

Next, we looked at Steve Jobs' ability to balance. To balance is to focus. Through his ability to find the balance in everything, he created a bridge between humanity and science, between artistry and technology.

In today's world, every company uses focus groups. They test the market, and try to learn what the consumer wants, but, in the end, they can't seem to beat what Jobs did without focus groups. You can't always hope to lead a market while you are being led by that market. That's what politicians do. There's a saying in real estate, "Know where everyone is going and get there first." The rationale is that when the others get there, you will already own the property, and you will make your money from that. That's what focus groups do – they let you in on the trend that people are creating and making.

Steve Jobs wasn't the kind of leader to follow the trends. He didn't really care about focus groups. So how did he look at products? How did he determine what products to take on? What products to refine? What features to incorporate?

Instead, Steve Jobs was the kind of leader we follow. He was the kind of leader Henry Ford spoke about when he talked about innovators. He was the kind of leader who shows us what is possible before we can even think of it. We did not anticipate the existence of the iPod until Jobs came up with it. We did not anticipate iTunes. Imagine if a focus group had been asked, "What do you want next, the CDROM or iTunes?" Many would have chosen the CDROM because the concept of an iTunes would have gone right over their heads. Now, iTunes is a major revenue earner for Apple.

Much of the work that Steve Jobs did while he was alive continues to reverberate through the lives of people around the world, whether consumer or competitor, whether Apple supporter or Apple detractor, or something between. Steve Jobs followed the dictates of his own vision, and played an infinite game that allowed Apple to break out of the limits of what was already available in the market to become the leader in human-friendly technologies.

If you enjoyed learning about Steve Jobs and found this book insightful, I would be forever grateful if you could leave a review. Reviews are the best way to help authors get feedback and help your fellow readers find the books worth reading. Thanks in advance!

Make sure to check out the other books in this 'Billionaire Visionaries' series:

Jeff Bezos: The Force Behind the Brand

Elon Musk: Moving the World One Technology at a Time

Bill Gates: The Man Behind Microsoft

Jack Ma: A Lesson in Trust, Honor, and Shared Prosperity

Richard Branson: The Force Behind Virgin